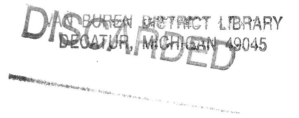

"More and more we must learn to think not in terms of race or color or language or religion or political boundaries, but in terms of humanity."

— Booker T. Washington

BOOKER T. WASHINGTON

BY DON TROY

GRAPHIC DESIGN
Robert E. Bonaker / Graphic Design & Consulting Co.

PROJECT COORDINATOR
James R. Rothaus / James R. Rothaus & Associates

EDITORIAL DIRECTION
Elizabeth Sirimarco

PHOTO RESEARCH
Ann Schwab / The Child's World, Inc.

COVER PHOTO
Portrait of Booker T. Washington / Archive Photos

CURRICULUM COORDINATOR
Cynthia Klingel / Curriculum Director, School District #77, Mankato, MN

Library of Congress Cataloging-in-Publication Data
Troy, Don
    Booker T. Washington / by Don Troy
      p. cm.
    Summary: Describes the life of Booker T. Washington, his
    accomplishments as an educator, and his impact on
            the fight for equality.
    ISBN 1-56766-556-X (library reinforced : alk. paper)

1. Washington, Booker T., 1856-1915—Juvenile literature.
2. Afro-Americans—Biography—Juvenile literature.
3. Educators—United States—Biography—Juvenile literature.
[1. Washington, Booker T., 1856-1915. 2. Educators. 3. Afro-
Americans—Biography.] I. Title

E185.97.W4T76 1998   98-4333
370'.92 — dc21   CIP
[B]   AC

Contents

Born a Slave

Booker T. Washington was born on April 5, 1856. His mother, Jane Burroughs, was an *African American*, and his father was an unknown White man. Booker and Jane lived on a large farm in Virginia, called a plantation, but they were not there by choice. Jane was a slave, which means that she was owned, like a piece of property, by the people who owned the plantation.

At that time, *slavery* was a common practice in the southern United States. Slave traders sailed to Africa and shipped captured African people to America on overcrowded cargo ships. Many of the slaves died either while resisting capture or during the journey. When the survivors reached America, they were sold at auctions. Farmers bought the slaves to work in tobacco and cotton fields or to do other hard labor.

Under this system, the slaves had no rights. They could be bought and sold at any time. They could not leave their masters, no matter how badly they were treated.

When Booker was born, his mother was a slave on the Burroughs plantation. Because he was born into slavery, Booker was owned by the Burroughs as well.

©1995 North Wind Pictures

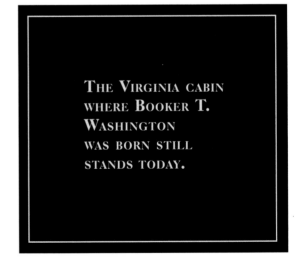

THE VIRGINIA CABIN WHERE BOOKER T. WASHINGTON WAS BORN STILL STANDS TODAY.

Hulton-Deutsch Collection/Corbis

THREE AFRICANS ABDUCTED FROM ABYSSINIA (PRESENT-DAY ETHIOPIA)
AWAIT THEIR FATE IN CHAINS.

A GROUP OF FREED SLAVES GATHERS ON THE PLANTATION OF A CONFEDERATE GENERAL DURING UNION OCCUPATION OF HIS PROPERTY.

When Booker was five years old, the southern states, including Virginia, tried to withdraw from the United States and form their own country, called the *Confederate States of America*. For the next four years, the northern and southern states fought the bitter American Civil War. Many thousands of people were killed.

In 1865, the *Union Army* of the northern states won the war, and the Confederates were forced to rejoin the United States. Slavery was outlawed throughout the nation. Booker and his family were free.

After the war, life was difficult in the South. Many farms had been destroyed in battle, and many farmers had been killed. Starting over was difficult, especially without the "free" labor the slaves had provided.

Life was especially difficult for the freed slaves. No one could afford to hire them because the plantation owners were poor themselves. There was little work available, and few slaves had been taught any real job skills. Just finding food, housing, and clothing was a struggle.

THE CIVIL WAR CHANGED THE FATE OF AFRICAN AMERICANS, BUT EVEN WITH THEIR NEW-FOUND FREEDOM, THEIR LIVES WERE NOT EASY.

Corbis-Bettmann

The Chance to Go to School

During the war, Booker's mother had married a man named Washington Ferguson, who had escaped from slavery. When the war ended, Booker and his family — including his brother, sister, and mother — went to live with Washington in Malden, West Virginia. Booker worked with his stepfather and brother in the salt and coal mines. It was hard work, but he was a hard worker.

Booker had always wanted to learn to read, but slaves were not allowed to go to school. At age 10, he pleaded with his parents to let him go to a new school for former slaves. His parents said he could go, as long as he kept working in the mines as well.

On the first day of school, the students were asked to stand and give their full names. He heard everyone else say two or three names, but he had never been called anything but Booker. He knew his stepfather and mother had the last name of Ferguson, but when his turn came, he gave his stepfather's first name as his last. "Booker Washington," he said.

That night, he and his mother talked about his name. She said that when he was born, she named him "Booker Taliaferro." That seemed difficult to spell, so he decided to use just his middle initial. For the rest of his life, he was known as Booker T. Washington.

FROM THE TIME HE WAS A CHILD, BOOKER WANTED TO
GO TO SCHOOL. HIS DESIRE TO GIVE OTHER AFRICAN
AMERICANS THE CHANCE TO LEARN WOULD BECOME
HIS LIFE'S WORK.

Tuskegee University Archives

"THE INDIVIDUAL WHO CAN DO SOMETHING THAT THE WORLD WANTS DONE WILL, IN THE END, MAKE HIS WAY REGARDLESS OF HIS RACE," BOOKER SAID. HIS BELIEF THAT BLACK STUDENTS SHOULD BE TAUGHT USEFUL SKILLS WAS THE INSPIRATION BEHIND TUSKEGEE INSTITUTE, THE ALABAMA SCHOOL BOOKER OPENED IN 1881. HERE, TUSKEGEE STUDENTS LEARN TO MAKE SHOES.

Booker was an outstanding student. At age 15, he left home to attend Virginia's Hampton Institute, a college for African Americans. At Hampton, students could work to pay for their education. Booker worked as a janitor. He later said, "I had to work late into the night, while at the same time I had to rise by four o'clock in the morning, in order to build the fires and have a little time in which to prepare my lessons."

One of Hampton's goals was to teach students "the dignity of labor," and Booker learned to love work. Years later he would say, "I have had no patience with any school which did not teach its students the dignity of labor."

Hampton also stressed the importance of self-reliance. Booker later argued that it was important for African Americans to acquire the skills necessary to live independently. All people, he believed, should be able to rely on themselves to meet the basic necessities of life.

After graduation, Booker returned home to Malden to teach at the local school. He was glad to have the opportunity to help the people in his hometown achieve more in their lives.

Hampton University Archives

NOT ONLY WAS BOOKER A STUDENT AT THE HAMPTON INSTITUTE, HE WAS LATER ASKED TO TEACH THERE.

Four years later, the head of the Hampton Institute invited Booker back to work in a new program. One hundred young Native American children had been invited to study at Hampton. The program turned out to be very successful. The Native Americans were excellent students.

Booker's next experiment at Hampton was to offer night classes for people who had to work during the day. Soon he had 25 new students.

Then, in 1881, a White banker and a Black leader from Tuskegee, Alabama, invited Booker to start a school for African Americans in their small, southern town. It seemed like an excellent opportunity, and Booker decided to take advantage of it. It turned out to be one of the most important decisions he ever made. At the Tuskegee Institute, Booker would find a forum where he could teach young African Americans the importance of being able to rely on their own skills and abilities.

Library of Congress

THE TUSKEGEE INSTITUTE PREPARED ITS STUDENTS FOR LIFE AFTER SCHOOL BY TEACHING SKILLS TO HELP THEM FIND WORK.

THE BLACKSMITH TRADE WAS AMONG THOSE TAUGHT AT TUSKEGEE. HERE, STUDENTS LEARN TO SHOE HORSES.

BOOKER T. WASHINGTON WAS ONLY **25** YEARS OLD IN **1881**, THE YEAR THE TUSKEGEE INSTITUTE OPENED ITS DOORS TO THE SCHOOL'S FIRST **30** STUDENTS.

Lessons at Tuskegee

When Booker arrived in Tuskegee, he was surprised to learn that there wasn't even a classroom, never mind a schoolhouse or campus. That did not stop him. He visited Alabama's small towns to recruit students. He found some African Americans who had already learned to read and were now teaching others. He invited these self-made teachers to come and be his students.

Then a local African American church donated a run-down shack. With 30 students, Booker began teaching in the old building on July 4th, 1881. The Tuskegee Institute was born.

Booker first had to decide which subjects to teach. English and math were obvious choices. Many other schools taught academic subjects like Latin, Greek, or philosophy. Would those be good choices for the Tuskegee Institute?

Booker considered his visits to the small Alabama towns where he had seen too many poor, hungry African Americans. What they needed most were food, shelter, and decent jobs. Booker's first concern was to make sure his students could find work to support themselves. Better still, he thought, many of them could go back to their towns to teach job skills to other African Americans.

Booker decided that subjects like Latin and philosophy would be useless for these particular students. He vowed that Tuskegee would teach practical subjects, such as how to grow crops and build houses. Food and shelter, he believed, must come first.

Before long, Booker decided to expand the school, but the land he wanted cost $500. Booker managed to borrow half the money from the Hampton Institute. Volunteers held festivals and church suppers to raise the rest.

To build a proper schoolhouse, the Tuskegee Institute needed bricks. The students learned how to dig clay, form bricks, and bake them in a kiln. The bricks were heavy, so Booker added classes on how to make wagons and wheelbarrows to carry them. The school needed furniture, too, so the students learned carpentry and upholstery skills. Soon Tuskegee added a print shop as well. Most of these practical, job-training courses began out of necessity.

Archive Photos

SINCE 1985, THE TUSKEGEE INSTITUTE HAS BEEN CALLED TUSKEGEE UNIVERSITY. MANY OF THE SCHOOL'S EARLY BUILDINGS ARE STILL IN USE TODAY.

Library of Congress

FROM MAKING BRICKS TO BUILDING WALLS, ALL THE TUSKEGEE STUDENTS CHIPPED IN TO BUILD THE INSTITUTE'S FIRST SCHOOLHOUSE.

Some students grumbled that they had come to school to study, not to push wheelbarrows full of bricks. But when they saw Booker himself shoveling clay and chopping wood, they followed his example.

Booker also insisted on teaching students the importance of discipline and personal cleanliness. He had been taught those values at Hampton. The Tuskegee students were required to bathe and brush their teeth every day and had morning neatness inspections.

Booker's own family life during this time was painful. He had married his childhood sweetheart, Fannie Smith, but she died just after giving birth to their daughter, Portia. Later he married another teacher, Olivia Davidson, but she died after having two sons, Booker, Jr., and Ernest.

Being a single parent was a difficult responsibility. Soon Booker married a third time. His new wife, Margaret, helped him provide a wonderful home for his children. Booker spent much of his time teaching, running the school, and raising money to keep the school going, but he was still devoted to his family.

Tuskegee University Archives

WASHINGTON MARRIED FANNIE SMITH IN 1882, BUT SHE DIED LESS THAN TWO YEARS LATER.

Tuskegee University Archives

THIS PHOTO OF BOOKER T. WASHINGTON'S FAMILY SHOWS (FROM LEFT TO RIGHT) HIS TWO SONS ERNEST DAVIDSON AND BOOKER T., JR., HIS THIRD WIFE MARGARET, BOOKER T., SR., AND HIS DAUGHTER PORTIA.

Integration or Segregation?

In 1895, Booker T. Washington became the first African American to speak to a White audience in the South. The occasion was a great *exposition*, the Cotton States and International Exposition in Atlanta.

Special exhibits came to Atlanta from all over the country. Philadelphia sent the Liberty Bell. Boston sent a model of the poet Longfellow's home. California set up a mining camp.

Anxious to encourage the North to do business with the South and to show that the Civil War was long behind them, the organizers invited Booker to speak. His speech would be so well received that he would become a nationally acclaimed spokesperson for Black Americans. Later on, however, some of his statements would be held against him.

Booker became somewhat nervous as he prepared his speech for the exposition. He was a confident speaker, and there was a great deal he wanted to say. But this was an extremely important speech — the first by a Black man to a White audience in the South. He knew many Whites hoped he would make a fool of himself. What should he say?

He thought long and hard about the situation in the South. Although African Americans had been granted certain rights after the Civil War ended, their lives were still difficult. Many Whites refused to see them as equals. Most areas of the South had *segregation* laws that kept Blacks and Whites apart. African Americans could not go to White schools or live in White neighborhoods. They could not serve on juries or marry Whites.

Atlanta History Center

THE GROUNDS OF COTTON STATES AND INTERNATIONAL EXPOSITION IN ATLANTA, GEORGIA. IT WAS AT THIS SITE WHERE BOOKER GAVE THE FAMOUS SPEECH THAT WAS LATER CALLED THE "ATLANTA COMPROMISE."

Corbis-Bettmann

WELL INTO THE 20TH CENTURY, ALMOST EVERYTHING WAS SEGREGATED IN THE SOUTH. AFRICAN AMERICANS HAD TO GO TO SEPARATE SCHOOLS, USE SEPARATE BATHROOMS, AND DRINK FROM SEPARATE DRINKING FOUNTAINS, ALONG WITH MANY OTHER SEGREGATED ACTIVITIES.

There were frequent acts of violence against Blacks as well. Some African Americans watched helplessly as their homes burned down. Others were beaten, or even illegally hung (called *lynching*) — merely because of their skin color. The Whites who committed these crimes were rarely punished.

Booker hated the segregation laws and knew they were wrong. He knew that his people were being denied their rights. Yet he also knew that if he seemed like a troublemaker to his White audience, he might be the last African American ever invited to make such a speech. He wanted to accomplish as much as possible, but he recognized that one speech would not convince the South to change its laws.

He was convinced that if African Americans had education and employment opportunities, they would achieve success and respect. Segregation would disappear as Whites began to recognize the contributions of their Black counterparts. He decided what to say: Segregation could be tolerated, for now, in the hope of gaining education and jobs for Blacks.

In the speech, Booker said that it would be "extremist folly" to agitate for *civil rights* at the present time. African Americans should be patient and concentrate first on education and jobs. Booker's speech is often called the "Atlanta Compromise." African Americans "compromised" by asking for less than they truly wanted, hoping to achieve a portion of their goals.

THE BODY OF A BLACK MAN HANGS FROM A TREE AT AN **1882** LYNCHING IN MINNESOTA.

Booker held his fingers apart above his head and said, "In all things that are purely social, we can be as separate as the fingers." Then he closed his fingers into a fist and added, "yet one as the hand in all things essential to mutual progress."

Many southerners in the audience had worried that Booker would use this speech to attack the segregation laws. They applauded loudly when he implied that segregation could be tolerated. The South had been hurting financially since the end of the Civil War. Southerners knew they needed African Americans in their work force, but they were not willing to give them social equality in return.

Many northerners had wanted to invest money in southern businesses, but they had seen racial tensions as a danger. They, too, applauded loudly at Booker's speech.

The speech made Booker famous. His new role would mean many hours of hard work and travel. It would also take him to the mansions of millionaires, to a famous New England university's campus, to the White House in Washington, and to the palace of the Queen of England. These opportunities helped Booker raise millions of dollars for education and job training at the Tuskegee Institute.

In 1896, Booker was given an honorary master's degree from Harvard, the nation's oldest university. He had come a long way since his childhood as an impoverished slave who dreamed of one day learning to read.

By 1899, after working for 17 years without a vacation, Booker was exhausted. He and his wife sailed to Europe, where England's Queen Victoria invited them to be her guest for tea at Windsor Castle.

Corbis-Bettmann

As time passed, Booker's fame grew. He was invited to travel around the country to speak at different events, often raising money for Tuskegee Institute.

Library of Congress

STUDENTS AT THE TUSKEGEE INSTITUTE LEARN TO MAKE MATTRESSES. BOOKER CONTINUED TO BELIEVE IT WAS IMPORTANT TO TEACH PEOPLE SKILLS THAT WOULD HELP THEM FIND WORK.

Was the Atlanta Compromise a Mistake?

More than a century later, some people still wonder whether Booker's "Atlanta Compromise" helped or hurt the cause of equality for African Americans. It is important to see the situation as he saw it at the time, when things were very different from today.

Booker was born a slave. To him freedom was wonderful in itself. He knew that African Americans did not have equal rights, and he believed that segregation was wrong. His first goal, however, was to see that Blacks had the basic necessities.

Booker felt it was more important to have food to eat than to eat that food with Whites. It was more important that a Black family could afford a home than whether that home was in a White neighborhood. He believed that the opportunity to get a good education was more important than whether all races attended the same schools.

Booker's famous compromise did not work out as he had expected. It may have helped rebuild business in the South. Factories opened, cotton and steel mills were built, and railroads were modernized. The South began to prosper again.

Unfortunately, African Americans were not able to enjoy this prosperity. Segregation kept them from the best work. In factories, they had the lowest-paying jobs. In cotton and steel mills, they could only work as janitors. On railroads, they were hired as porters, not as engineers or brakemen. Now other African Americans criticized Booker, arguing that he had been wrong.

One of these critics was W. E. B. Du Bois, another well-known African American leader. His background was different from Booker's. He had been born in the North, in Massachusetts, after the end of the Civil War and slavery. Du Bois argued that Booker had been wrong to compromise. He said segregation must not be tolerated, no matter what the cost.

Du Bois was also well educated, having graduated from Fisk and Harvard Universities. He argued that Tuskegee should be teaching academic courses instead of *vocational skills*. He believed this would create more highly educated leaders in the African American community.

Booker still believed his choices had been good ones. In 1896, for example, Tuskegee had hired the first African American graduate of Iowa State College. His name was George Washington Carver.

For 47 years, Carver taught Tuskegee students and southern farmers how to grow bigger and better crops. He invented new uses for sweet potatoes and peanuts. He was given many awards for science, including one from President Franklin Roosevelt in 1939.

Still, criticism of Booker's ideas was growing. Believing that patience with segregation was not working, a group of African Americans formed a new organization in 1910 to fight for civil rights. They named the group the *National Association for the Advancement of Colored People*. (At that time, African Americans were often called "colored people" or "Negroes.") The organization became better known by its initials, the NAACP.

Over time, the NAACP became very powerful. As one of its leaders, W. E. B. Du Bois soon replaced Booker as the best-known spokesperson for African Americans.

WILLIAM EDWARD BURGHARDT DU BOIS WAS BORN IN 1868. HIS LIFE WAS DIFFERENT FROM THAT OF BOOKER T. WASHINGTON, AND HE NEVER EXPERIENCED WHAT AFRICAN AMERICANS IN THE SOUTH HAD LIVED THROUGH BEFORE THE CIVIL WAR.

EQUALITY

As a spokesperson for African Americans, Booker was asked for advice by three United States presidents, William McKinley, Theodore Roosevelt, and William Howard Taft. He is shown here with President Roosevelt in 1901.

In Terms of Humanity

In 1901, Booker wrote his auto-biography, *Up from Slavery*. One review called the moving story "one of the most cheerful, hopeful books that we have had the privilege to read."

Among the readers were wealthy northerners who had never thought much about the education of former slaves. Millionaires George Eastman, the camera maker, and Andrew Carnegie, the steel manufacturer, were among those impressed with Booker's story. After Eastman read the book, he sent Booker $5,000 to help with the education of African Americans. Later Eastman would contribute $250,000 to the Tuskegee Memorial Fund. Carnegie gave Booker $600,000 for Tuskegee.

That same year, Booker was invited to dine with President Theodore Roosevelt at the White House.

Many southerners were shocked. Their segregation laws still did not allow Blacks and Whites to eat together.

By 1911, however, President William Howard Taft had begun to remove almost all African Americans from government positions. When President Woodrow Wilson was elected in 1912, he continued to promote Taft's policies. Strict segregation was enforced in many branches of the federal government. All African Americans who had jobs in the United States Postal Service, for example, were let go.

There had been more than 1,000 known lynchings between 1900 and 1914 in the South. Good jobs were difficult to come by for African Americans, and segregation was still a fact of life. Booker began to believe that much more needed to be done.

He wrote a strongly worded article titled, "Is the Negro Having a Fair Chance?" He argued against segregation on the railroads, lynchings, interference with the right of Black men to vote, and the difficulty getting an education that African Americans still faced. Even W. E. B. Du Bois was pleased with Booker's frankness. As President Wilson's segregation practices continued, Booker lashed out against *racism* more strongly than ever.

By 1913, Booker realized that segregation had caused racism to increase. Many African Americans had gotten better educations and jobs because of his efforts, but little progress had been made toward equality with Whites.

Booker continued to work as hard as ever. He wrote a number of books and articles. He continued to work with the National Negro Business League, which he had founded a decade earlier to encourage the growth of Black-owned businesses. Booker also continued to pour much of his time and efforts into his beloved Tuskegee Institute.

In November 1915, Booker's health finally gave out. Many people said he had simply worked himself to death. He was in New York making speeches and raising money for Tuskegee when he was hospitalized. After a week in the hospital, Booker realized he was dying.

He and his wife took the train to Tuskegee that same afternoon, arriving home in the evening. "I was born in the South," said Washington. "I have lived and labored in the South. I expect to die in the South." He died the following morning, on November 13, 1915. He was only 59 years old.

When Booker was buried at Tuskegee, people around the country mourned his death. The United States had lost one of its most powerful and respected African American leaders.

Booker T. Washington devoted his life to helping African Americans establish themselves as equals in the United States. "More and more," he once said, "we must learn not to think in terms of race or color or political boundaries, but in terms of humanity."

National Negro Business League.
Executive Committee.

BOOKER FOUNDED THE NATIONAL NEGRO BUSINESS LEAGUE IN 1900 TO HELP ENCOURAGE THE GROWTH OF BLACK-OWNED BUSINESSES. HE CONTINUED TO SUPPORT THE LEAGUE UNTIL HIS DEATH, ALTHOUGH HE WAS DISCOURAGED BY THE FACT THAT AFRICAN AMERICANS SELDOM HAD SUFFICIENT RESOURCES TO START A BUSINESS. BOOKER (FIRST ROW, SECOND FROM THE LEFT) IS SHOWN HERE WITH THE ORGANIZATION'S EXECUTIVE COMMITTEE.

UPI/Corbis-Bettmann

IN 1941, THE FIRST SCHOOL TO TRAIN AFRICAN AMERICANS AS OFFICERS IN THE U.S. AIR CORPS OPENED ITS DOORS IN TUSKEGEE. STANDING IN THE SHADOW OF THE BOOKER T. WASHINGTON MONUMENT, MAJOR GENERAL WALTER R. WEAVER DELIVERS THE INAUGURAL ADDRESS AT THE DEDICATION OF THE 99TH PURSUIT SQUADRON AND PILOT TRAINING SCHOOL.

Timeline

1856	Booker T. Washington is born in Virginia.
1865	The American Civil War ends, and African American slaves are freed.
1866	Washington goes to school to begin his education.
1872	Washington leaves home to attend the Hampton Institute, a three-year college for African Americans.
1881	Washington begins teaching a class of 30 students at the Tuskegee Institute in Alabama.
1895	The Cotton States and International Exposition is held in Atlanta. Washington is asked to speak, and his speech is later called the "Atlanta Compromise."
1896	Washington is granted an honorary master's degree from Harvard University.
1899	Washington and his wife sail to Europe. He is invited to meet with the Queen of England.
1900	Washington organizes the National Negro Business League.
1901	Washington writes his autobiography, *Up from Slavery*. The book interests many wealthy northerners, who give money to the Tuskegee Institute.
1903	President Theodore Roosevelt invites Washington to the White House to dine with him.
1910	The National Association for the Advancement of Colored People is founded by W. E. B. Du Bois and other Black leaders.
1911	President William Howard Taft removes African Americans from government jobs. His successor, President Woodrow Wilson, continues this policy.
1915	Washington becomes ill. He dies on November 13, 1915, in Tuskegee, Alabama.

Glossary

African American
Americans whose ancestors came from the African continent. In the past, African Americans were called colored people and Negros.

civil rights
The rights of people guaranteed by law. United States citizens are guaranteed certain rights by the Constitution and its amendments.

Confederate States of America
The name given to the southern states that withdrew from the United States of America to become a separate country at the time of the American Civil War.

exposition
A public exhibition or show.

lynching
The act of putting someone to death (usually by hanging) without legal consent.

National Association for the Advancement of Colored People (NAACP)
An organization formed in 1910 to fight for African Americans' civil rights.

racism
The belief that one race is superior to another.

segregation
The separation or isolation of a race, class, or ethnic group.

slavery
The practice of forcing a person or group of people to work for others without pay.

Union Army
The army of the the United States (the northern states) during the American Civil War.

vocational skills
Skills that an individual can use at work.

Index

For Further Information

Washington, Booker T. *Up from Slavery: An Autobiography* (editions available from several publishers).

Nicholson, Lois P. *Booker T. Washington* (Junior Black Americans of Achievement). Broomall, PA: Chelsea House, 1997.

McKissack, Pat, et. al. *Booker T. Washington: Leader and Educator.* Springfield, NJ: Enslow Publishers, Inc., 1992.

The following websites offer more information about Booker T. Washington and the Tuskegee Institute:
http://www.nps.gov/bowa
http://www.nps.gov/tuin

About the Author

Don Troy was born and raised in Boston, Massachusetts. He received his Ph.D from Boston University in 1971 and was Certified as a Total Family Therapist by Boston Family Institute in 1973.

He taught at Stonehill College in Massachusetts from 1963 to 1973. Moving to California in 1973, he spent four years as director of a national trade association for marriage and family educators and counsellors.